The Archbishop's
School of Christianity and Science

Written by John Po

❦ ❦ ❦

Section 1 *Friends or e.*

I spent half my life working as a scientist in Cambridge, and I've spent the second half of my life as a Christian minister. People hearing that sometimes look at me as if I'm a bit odd, rather like being a vegetarian butcher. I want to try to explain why I think that Christianity and science are really friends and they are not, as some people seem to think, at each other's throats. The fact of the matter is that they need each other because each, in its own way, is concerned with trying to find out the truth about the world in which we live.

The birth of science

Science as we know it today started up almost four hundred years ago in Europe, with the discoveries of people like Galileo and, later, Isaac Newton. Why did it begin then and there, and not in ancient Greece, where people were very clever and very curious, or in medieval China, whose civilisation was in many ways ahead of that of Europe? Quite a lot of people think that the answer lies in the influence of Christian thinking. If the rational God is behind creation, the world will be orderly, having a pattern to it. Yet to discover that pattern requires us to look and see, since no one tells God what to do – the form of creation was a divine free choice.

Recognising that there would be a pattern pointed those early scientists to the use of mathematics. That subject is concerned with studying possible kinds of patterns, but the fact that the pattern had been freely chosen meant you had to use experiment and observation to find out exactly what God had decided to do. Put these two ideas together and you have what it takes to get modern science going. The Christian doctrine of creation was the midwife that brought science to birth. It would be odd then if there were a real conflict between the two. Of course there have been problems between them at times, as there can be in any friendship. For instance, Galileo

---

certainly had his troubles with the Church authorities, but he was also a genuinely religious man, as were most of the other founding figures of science. Christianity and science are friends and not enemies.

All the answers?

But doesn't science tell us all we need to know, giving us enough answers to mean that we don't have any need of religion as well? Not at all. Science doesn't even ask all the questions. It has been very successful precisely by not trying to ask and answer every possible query. It limits itself to asking *how* things happen. Science's task is to explore the processes of the world that keep things going. On its part, religion is asking another and deeper set of questions, enquiring into *why* things are happening. Is there a meaning and a purpose behind it all?

"Religion without science is blind. Science without religion is lame. 99

(Albert Einstein)

We know perfectly well that we can and should ask both types of question. You come into my kitchen and the kettle is boiling. I put on my scientific hat and I say to you that this is because the burning gas generates heat, which raises the temperature of the water to 100° centigrade and then it boils. That is certainly true, and in its way worth knowing. Yet nothing prevents me taking off my scientific hat and saying that the kettle is boiling because I want to make a cup of tea, and would you like to have one too? We need to ask and answer both the how and the why questions in order properly to understand what is going on. I like to think that I am two-eyed and that, by using both my scientific eye and my religious eye, I can see more than I could with either alone.

Search for truth

The most important religious issue is the question of truth. Christian faith can comfort us in life and at the approach of death, but it cannot really do either of these things unless it is actually true. People sometimes say that science deals with facts and that religion deals with opinions. Actually that involves making two bad mistakes, one about science and one about Christianity.

First, there are no interesting scientific facts that are not already interpreted facts, and interpretation always involves theoretical opinion about how the apparatus being used actually works. Second, there are reasons for religious beliefs, just as there are reasons for scientific beliefs. Faith does not mean shutting your eyes, gritting your teeth and believing six impossible things before breakfast just because some unquestionable religious authority tells you that is what you have to do. If faith involved intellectual suicide, I couldn't be a Christian. Faith calls for commitment, but the leap is into the light and not into the dark.

Of course there are also some important differences between the way we figure out things in science and the way we do in religion. Science treats the world as an object, as an 'it', something that you can manipulate and pull apart to find out what it is made of. That gives science its great secret weapon: experiment. However, in the realm of personal experience, whether we are encountering each other or encountering God, testing has to give way to trusting. If I am always setting little traps to see if you are my friend, I shall destroy the possibility of friendship between us. It is just a fact of the spiritual life that God is not to be put to the test in an impersonal experimental way. But that doesn't mean that there are not other ways of learning about God, for God acts to make himself known to us. We shall see that some of them are even helped by science's understanding of the universe.

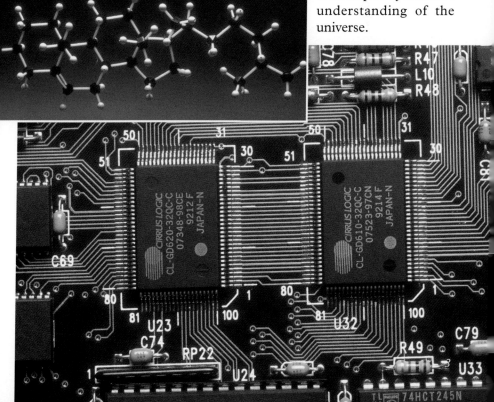

Section 2 *Is there Anybody there?*

We might expect to be able to learn something about God from the study of creation. That doesn't mean that the universe will be full of things stamped 'Made by God', but we might anticipate that we should find some hints that a divine mind and will lies behind its history. Can science help us to answer the question, 'Is there Anybody out there?'? I think it can.

In the beginning ... The first thing to be clear about is that the religious idea of creation is not simply about how things began. God's role is not just to light the blue touch paper of the Big Bang and then retire. God is as much the Creator today as God was fourteen billion years ago. It is certainly very interesting that the universe as we know it had a beginning, even if, as Stephen Hawking thinks, it was rather a fuzzy one. Even more important, however, is the fact that it has had a long and fruitful history since then, during which the Creator's purposes have been unfolding. It all started very simple, the universe post-Big Bang being just an expanding ball of energy. Fourteen billion years later, the world is very rich and complicated, with beings like ourselves in it. That astonishing fruitfulness might itself suggest that something has been going on in cosmic history beyond merely one thing after another. So let us think in a little more detail about what our universe is like.

Why is science possible?

The universe is wonderfully understandable. We can make sense of it, and this is what makes science possible. Mostly we tend to take this for granted, but actually it is a very significant and surprising fact about the world. Of course, we have to be able to make sense of everyday things in order to be able to survive, but that doesn't mean that we have to be able to understand how the stars work (they are far too big and remote for us to be able to do anything about them) or how atoms behave (too small). When Sherlock Holmes first meets Dr Watson, the great investigator pretends that he does not know if the Earth goes round the Sun or vice-versa. When Watson is horrified, Holmes simply says, 'What does it matter for my daily work as a detective?'. It doesn't, but we know many things that are more than just mundane aids to survival.

Not only is the universe deeply intelligible, but it is also beautiful in the marvellous patterns of its order. 'Wonder' is a word that scientists often use, for it is the pay-off for all the many hours of weary labour involved in scientific research. As we explore the universe, we find that it is a world that seems, as it were, shot through with signs of mind. Is this just our luck, or is it a clue pointing to a deep significance? It is not an unreasonable thought that the rational beauty of the universe is a reflection of the Mind of its Creator. I

> " *Either God is everywhere present in nature or He is nowhere.* "
>
> *(Aubrey Moore, arguing that God creates through evolutionary process and not through occasional acts)*

actually believe that science is possible because the world is a creation and we are creatures made in the image of our Creator.

Creatures of stardust

God is not a God in a hurry, and the pace of creation has been sure and steady. It took about ten billion years from the Big Bang for life to develop on Earth, and a further three to four billion years for it to result in self-conscious beings like ourselves. Yet in recent years scientists have come to realise that the potentiality for these happenings was built into the universe from the start. The world was pregnant with life from the Big Bang onwards. It turns out that it is not just any old universe that is capable of producing carbon-based life, but only one that is very special in its character. Its laws of nature have to be finely tuned if life is to be a possibility at all.

Let me give you just one example, chosen from many possibilities, of why we think that this is so. The chemistry of life is the chemistry of carbon. Yet, because the very early universe was very simple, it only had very simple constituents, in chemical terms just hydrogen and helium. So where has the carbon come from? There is only one place where it can be made, in the nuclear furnaces of the stars. Every atom of carbon in our bodies was once inside a star – we are creatures made of stardust.

It turns out, however, that it is very difficult to make carbon out of helium. In fact, it is only possible at all because of a remarkable coincidence in the exact form of the laws of nuclear physics. This results in an enhancing effect (we call it a resonance) occurring at precisely the right energy to make carbon production possible. Without this coincidence there would be no life anywhere at all. So is this just our luck, or is it a sign that the universe is indeed not just any old world, but a creation whose laws have been chosen by its Creator precisely to allow it to have a fruitful history? I think it is the latter, a hint that God's purposes lie behind cosmic history.

A thinking universe

What is the most astonishing thing that has happened over the fourteen billion years since the Big Bang? I think it is the dawning of self-conscious life here on Earth. In our ancestors the universe became aware of itself. A great French thinker, Blaise Pascal, once said that human beings, small and frail as we are in comparison with the vast scale of the universe, are nevertheless greater than all the stars, for we know them and

> *"The more I examine the universe, the more evidence I find that the universe in some sense must have known we were coming.* **,,**
> *(Freeman Dyson, a distinguished physicist)*

ourselves and they know nothing. This suggests to me that there is something specially significant about persons and that it is reasonable to believe that there is a divine Person whose will has been behind that amazing development in the universe's history.

Evolution

The way that life developed was through a long evolutionary process that turned a world in which at first there were only bacteria, into a world containing thinking beings. Some people believe that it was a death blow to religion when Charles Darwin, in 1859, made it clear that evolution played this role. They see this as the final victory in the battle between scientific light and religious darkness. Such a view is not only tendentious, it is historically ignorant. Just as there were scientists in 1859 who had difficulties with Darwin's idea, so there were clergymen who welcomed these new insights. One of them was Charles Kingsley, who coined the phrase that admirably expresses how to think theologically about evolution. Kingsley said that God could no doubt have produced a ready-made universe, but instead he had done something cleverer than that in bringing into being an evolving world, which is a creation 'allowed to make itself'. If creation is the act of the God of love, it will not be a world in which God is a kind of cosmic tyrant, doing absolutely everything and leaving no freedom for creatures to be themselves, and even to make themselves. I find this way of thinking a deeply satisfying way to combine the scientific insights of evolution with a Christian understanding of creation.

Section 3 **Can a scientist pray?**

We call God 'Father', not because we think he is an old man with a white beard who lives in the sky, but because the personal language of Father is more accurate than the impersonal language of 'Force' would be. Human words are inadequate to catch the infinite reality of God, but personal metaphors are simply the best we have. Their use implies that we expect

God to do particular things in particular situations. In other words, if God is Father he must act within the unfolding history of the world, as indeed the Bible portrays God as doing. But can we really believe this today, when science describes a world of such great regularity? Don't things just happen? Putting it bluntly, could a scientist pray, actually expecting that God might do something in response?

Storms and butterflies

In actual fact, the science of the twentieth century has completely changed the kind of clockwork understanding of the world that Newtonian science might have seemed to suggest. Instead, today we have a picture that is more subtle and, I believe, more supple than that. It all started with atoms. Quantum theory tells us that one cannot predict their behaviour – they might do this or they might do that. Then people found out that even the physical world at the level of everyday experience is by no means as predictable as we had thought it to be. There are some 'clocks' around, but there are also an awful lot of 'clouds'. By the latter I mean systems that are so extremely sensitive that the tiniest disturbance will totally change their future behaviour. This discovery is called *chaos theory*, and one of the ways in which it came to light was through thinking about the weather. A popular way of expressing this insight is to talk about 'the butterfly effect'. Weather systems can be so sensitive that a butterfly stirring the air in the African jungle today could cause effects that grow and grow until they produce a storm over Britain in about three weeks' time. Detailed long-term weather forecasting is never going to work – we just can't know about all those butterflies!

> *"I notice that when I pray, coincidences happen more frequently."*
> (Archbishop William Temple)

An open universe

How should we think about this astonishing degree of inbuilt unpredictability present in nature? I think that we should see it as a sign that the universe is open to its future. By that I mean that the kind of causes that physics describes are only a part of the story of what makes things happen. Actually, we know that must be true, because we ourselves experience the power to act as agents in the world. When I raise my arm, there is a bits and pieces account of how my muscles contract, but there is also my decision to do so, which is an act of me as a whole person. And if we can act to bring about the future, it scarcely seems incredible that God can also play a part

> "Ask and it will be given you; search and you will find."
>
> (Matthew 7:7)

in forming creation's future. It is perfectly sensible for me to take science seriously and also to believe in divine providential action in history.

Why pray?

If what I have been saying is right, a scientist certainly can pray, but why do we have actually to ask God for things? God knows everything, so why doesn't he just get on with it? Do we have to make a fuss to goad God into action? Of course not. I think one reason why we are told to pray is that in doing so we offer our little bit of power to influence the future, to be taken by God, together with his much greater power, and used to the greatest effect. Things become possible when human and divine wills are aligned that would not be possible when they are at cross-purposes with each other. It is rather like laser light. It has remarkable properties because it is what the physicists call 'coherent'. This means that all its waves are in step with each other, so that all the crests coincide with maximum effect. In prayer we are seeking a laser-like coherence between human will and divine will.

Life's mystery

Prayer is effective, but it is not magic. It doesn't involve just filling out a blank cheque given us by our heavenly Father Christmas. That is why prayer has to be in the spirit of 'Thy will be done'. There is no escaping the mystery of individual human life. If people pray for the healing of a very sick person, they are really asking that that person may receive wholeness through what is happening to them. This may come through physical recovery, but it may also come through that person being given the grace to accept the imminent destiny of death. No one can tell beforehand what form healing will take.★

Section 4 What about miracles?

It is one thing to believe that God acts within the open grain of nature. It is quite another thing to believe that God has done such a totally unprecedented thing as to raise a man from death to new and unending life. The resurrection of Jesus is a miracle in the strict sense of its being an astonishing event, totally outside any kind of natural expectation. Can we

---

★Note: A fuller consideration of the many facets of prayer can be found in *The Archbishop's School of Prayer.*

---

who live in a scientific age, believe in that sort of thing? That is a very serious question for Christianity, since the resurrection is the pivot on which so much Christian belief turns.

God: faithful but not boring

Miracles, if they happen, are one-off events and so science, which is concerned with what usually happens, cannot do much more than underline the fact that they are contrary to normal expectation. The real problem in believing in miracles is actually theological rather than scientific. One thing that would be really incredible about God is that he is a kind of celestial conjurer, a show-off who does a trick today that he didn't think of doing yesterday and won't be bothered to do tomorrow. That kind of capricious God makes no theological sense at all.

The problem of miracle is the problem of divine consistency. We can be sure that God is totally reliable, but with the consistency of a person and not with the uniformity of a force. Gravity is always the same in an unchanging sort of way, but people can be consistent without being condemned to a boring sameness. They do particular things in

> "God does not shake miracles at Nature at random as if from a pepper-castor. They come on great occasions; they are found at the ganglia of history."
>
> (C.S. Lewis)

particular circumstances, and unexpected things in unprecedented circumstances. So if God does something totally new – as Christians believe he did in raising Jesus from the dead – that can make perfect sense if we can see that something unprecedented was going on that brought with it these wholly novel consequences. Of course, that is just what Christians do believe about Jesus, for we think that God was present in him in a totally unique way.

The resurrection of Jesus

Jesus died a miserable death, painful and shameful and deserted by his followers. It looks like a total failure. I actually believe that if that were the end of the story of Jesus, we would never have heard of him. Yet the fact is that the story of Jesus continued beyond that awful death; I believe that this is because he was indeed raised from the dead on the first Easter Day. That belief makes sense because it involves a three-fold vindication:

● It vindicates Jesus. It was not fitting that his wonderful life should end in failure.

● It vindicates God. The cross puts a question mark not only over Jesus, but also over God, his Father. Did God abandon the one man who

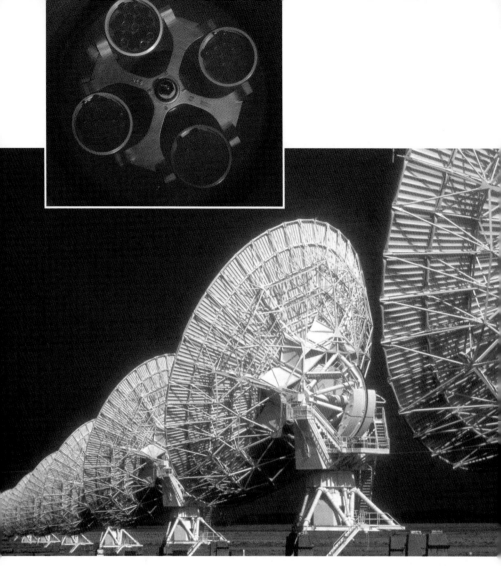

wholly committed himself to obedience to the divine will? Easter shows us that God did not.

- It vindicates a deep-seated human intuition that the last word about life does not lie with death. Christians believe that Jesus' resurrection within history is the foretaste and guarantee of what awaits all of us beyond history. Paul told the Corinthians 'as all die in Adam, so all will be made alive in Christ' (1 Cor. 15:22). There is much more that one could say about the resurrection, but these simple ideas indicate how a scientist can begin to make sense of such an astonishing belief.

Section 5 *How will it end?*

The universe as we see it today is orderly and fruitful, but how will it end? If the world truly makes sense, it must have a final fulfilment as well as a present fertility. Here is an important issue in the interaction between science and religion.

Futility

Scientists do not only peer into the past towards the Big Bang; they also peer into the future. On the largest scale, the history of the universe is a closely balanced tug-of-war between the explosive effects of the Big Bang, driving matter apart, and the tug of gravity, pulling matter together. Whichever wins, the end will be futility. The ultimate fate of the universe is either cold decay (if expansion wins) or fiery collapse (if gravity wins). Faced with the futility of freeze or fry, how can we claim that the world makes sense?

This is a serious challenge to Christianity, but I do not think it is any more serious than the even more certain knowledge of our individual deaths. The atheist physicist, Steven Weinberg, said that the more he understood the universe, the more it seemed pointless to him. Was he right?

Life after death

If Weinberg was wrong, and the world does make sense after all, that must be because, for us and for the universe, there is a destiny beyond death. Science can only be silent about that possibility, for there is no natural expectation that this is the case, but science's story is not the only story to be told. The Christian story can take us beyond the blank wall of mortality that stops science short. Jesus dealt directly with this issue in an argument he had with the Sadducees (Mark 12:18-27). They did not believe in a destiny beyond death, but Jesus reminded them of what God had said to Moses at the burning bush: 'I am the God of Abraham, the God of Isaac and the God of Jacob'. He then commented, 'The God not of the dead, but of the living'.

> *"For the creation waits with eager longing for the revealing of the children of God; for the creation was subjected to futility, not of its own will but of the will of the one who subjected, in hope that the creation itself will be set free from its bondage to decay and will attain the freedom of the glory of the children of God. "*
>
> *(Romans 8:19-21)*

In other words, if the Patriarchs mattered to God once, and they certainly did, then they matter to the faithful God for ever. If we matter to God once, and we do, then we shall matter to God for ever. There is no natural hope of a destiny beyond death, but nevertheless there is every hope, because it depends on the utter faithfulness of God.

The new creation

What that life will be like is hard for us to understand. (You might well say, 'Wait and see'.) Our best clue is given us by the risen Christ. It is indeed Jesus who returns from death, bearing the scars of his passion. Yet he is not just resuscitated, made alive again in order to die again. Jesus is transformed, living a new and glorified life, so that he can appear and disappear at will. The life that will await us beyond death is not just more of this kind of life, but it will be the life of God's new creation, that has already begun to grow from the seed-event of Christ's resurrection. This world exists at some distance from its Creator, as it is allowed to be itself and to make itself; that world will be fully integrated with God's life and energy. Its life will be a process of unending fulfilment, as the inexhaustible resources of the divine nature are made continually accessible to us.

One world ...

I passionately believe in the unity of knowledge. As a physicist and a priest I want to hold together the insights of science and the insights of Christianity as I think about the rich world of created reality. I hope this book shows a little of how this can be done with intellectual integrity and respect. There is fruitful exchange between science and Christianity, two great aspects of the single human search for truth.

OTHER BOOKS BY JOHN POLKINGHORNE

A complete list of John's books is available from any SPCK Bookshop.

- *The Way The World Is* (SPCK: Triangle)
- *Quarks, Chaos and Christianity* (SPCK: Triangle)
- *Searching for Truth* (Bible Reading Fellowship)
- *Belief in God in an Age of Science* (Yale University Press)

For an AUDIO TAPE featuring John Polkinghorne, see next page.
